Costumes of the
Seventeenth and Eighteenth Century

Costumes of the Seventeenth and Eighteenth Century

PHILLIS CUNNINGTON

Publishers

PLAYS, INC.

Boston

First published in 1970
by Faber and Faber Limited
3 Queen Square London WC1
© Phillis Cunnington 1968
First American edition published by
Plays, Inc. 1970
Reprinted 1973

Published in Great Britain under the title
Your Book of Seventeenth and
Eighteenth Century Costume

Library of Congress Catalog Card Number
70–115950

International Standard Book Number
0–8238–0086–5

Printed in Great Britain

ACKNOWLEDGEMENTS

A number of the drawings are taken from *Handbook of English Costume in the Seventeenth Century* and *Handbook of English Costume in the Eighteenth Century* by C. Willett Cunnington and Phillis Cunnington, published by Plays, Inc.

CONTENTS

9

CONTENTS

9

17th Century

Horse fly

08/11/73

INTRODUCTION

The fashions of the late 16th century continued, with modifications, all through the reign of James I.

With the purer taste of Charles I, both men's and women's clothes became less bulky and a little less ornamental.

Woollen textiles of a superior quality began to be used for gentlemen's suits, the coarser fabrics being left for the workers.

Although the Puritans had a preference for dark colours, their political leaders might be as brightly dressed as the Royalists, red being a favourite colour.

However, dark clothes at this time did become fashionable. We are told by a writer in 1630 that when a gentleman 'went up to London, he was to be new clothed after the English fashion which was then black clothes'.[1] Blue was avoided by gentlemen, since blue coats were worn by serving men and apprentices.

Decoration of men's clothes by slashing and 'paning' (long slashes) went out of fashion by 1650 and was largely replaced by ribbon trimming, especially for men. On a surviving specimen, at the Victoria and Albert Museum, 72 yards of ribbon in loops were measured.

Women's clothes too became less cumbersome after the farthingale (the hooped petticoat) was given up in the 1620's, but a corset-like bodice with tight lacing to produce a small waist was a marked feature from about 1650.

[1] Memoirs of Marmaduke Rawdon (Pub. by the Camden Society. 1863).

MEN'S CLOTHES

1600–1665

The doublet was a man's body wear until about 1665 (Fig. 1).

At first it was close-fitting, padded and stiffened with canvas or buckram. It had a high stand collar and a skirt cut in tabs which, after about 1610, sloped down to a point in front. A belt or a shoulder belt or sash might be worn. The doublet was fastened down the front with buttons or with ties called 'points' or very rarely with hooks and eyes. The sleeves were close and often slashed down the inner side to show an elegant shirt sleeve (*see* Fig. 9) or 'paned' above the elbow (Fig. 2). *Wings*, which were a kind of fancy epaulettes covering the shoulder seam, were usual for doublets and jerkins during the first half of the century.

From the 1630's doublets were short and comparatively plain.

Working men's doublets, however, were loose, like thigh-length jackets with belts. Later in the century they were called 'jumps' (*see* Fig. 19).

The jerkin, sometimes called a jacket, was fashionable until 1630 (Fig. 3). It was worn over the doublet but was not an outdoor garment. It was made like the doublet but was often sleeveless with wings only. Sometimes sham hanging sleeves, now mere streamers, were added.

The gown was a long loose garment open down the front (Fig. 4). It usually had true 'hanging sleeves' which were very long

14

and tubular with an opening at elbow level through which the arm could emerge for practical purposes. The gown was worn over the doublet, but chiefly by the learned professions and state officials.

A man's neck wear was either a collar, called a band or a ruff. Both collars and ruffs were sewn to a plain deep neckband which fitted inside the doublet collar and both were usually starched white though sometimes yellow starch was used.

Ruffs were set in tubular folds radiating out from the neck with a figure-of-eight appearance round the edge. They were often made in several layers. For men they were usually closed all round (Fig. 5).

The collar or band was either turned down all round and called a *falling band*, or raised round the back of the head with the straight edges meeting under the chin and called a *standing band*. They were tied in front with tasselled cords called band strings. Ruffs too could be falling or standing. There were two methods used to keep them standing; one was a wire frame attached to the neck of the doublet behind, and called a *supportasse* or *under propper*; the other was a tabbed stiffened attachment at the back, called a *Pickadil* or *Pickadilly*.

An unfortunate thing happened to one gentleman in 1620.

> 'Then for two lice (I will be sworne he found)
> upon my Pickadilly creeping round.'[1]

At the wrist, hand ruffs, now called ruffles or turn-back cuffs, were worn. Collars and cuffs were usually edged with lace.

[1] S. Rowlands, *The Night Raven*.

15

LEG WEAR

Trunk hose consisted of an upper breeches portion distended with padding called bombast and a lower hose or tailored stocking portion, this forming a single garment (Fig. 6). Sometimes the hose portion, *canions*, ended near the knees and then separate stockings were drawn up over them. Trunk hose went out of fashion by 1620 except for ceremonial wear.

Breeches in varying styles were worn throughout the 17th century. There were two main kinds, those gathered in and fastened above or below the knee and those left open below (like shorts).

Knee breeches fastened below the knee and called *Venetians* were worn from 1570 to 1620 (Fig. 7).

Cloak bag breeches were popular until about the 1630's (Fig. 8). They were very full and gathered in above the knee and there trimmed with ornamental metal tags called *aglets* or with masses of ribbon loops called *fancies*. This trimming was not often added to workmen's breeches. Breeches open below were of two sorts. The long ones ending below the knee were called *Spanish breeches*. They were very fashionable from 1630–45 and came back into fashion again in Charles II's reign (Fig. 9). Labourers wore these so long that they looked like trousers, but trousers did not come into fashion until the 19th century. Those that were short, ending above the knee, sometimes like modern shorts, were known as *Dutch breeches* (*see* Figs. 10, 12 and 41). They were very popular from 1600–10. James I wore them and they became fashionable again from the 1640's to the 1670's.

On their feet men wore boots or shoes, the heel being raised for the first time in 1600 (Fig. 11). Red heels were worn only with full dress and continued for Court wear to the end of the 18th century. Large rosettes of ribbon or lace, called *shoe roses*, were a favourite form of decoration for shoes from 1610 to 1680. Square toes were fashionable from about 1635.

Boots ending above or below the knee, where they had cup-shaped tops, were usually worn for riding, but boots with spurs soon became fashionable for walking and formed part of a gentleman's outdoor wear.

Startups were boots reaching to or just above the ankle, made of rough leather and generally worn by country folk and labourers.

Overshoes called *pantofles* and shaped like mules were fashionable till about 1650.

Tailored stockings made from material cut on the cross were still in use but by now most people were wearing knitted stockings. Dandies with thin legs wore false calves under the stockings.

'They say he puts off the calves of his legs with stockings every night.'[1]   1601

Boot hose or *stirrup hose* were stockings worn over a finer pair to protect it from damage inside the boot.

Boot-hose tops were decorated borders to the boot hose and were always turned out for display.

Out of doors, *cloaks* were worn—some were short, some knee-length, some had capes and some had sleeves (Fig. 12).

A gaberdine was a long loose overcoat with wide sleeves and because of its width was sometimes called a cloak. It was often worn on horseback (Fig. 13). It was also defined by a contemporary as 'a cloake of felt for raynie weather'.[2]

[1] Ben Jonson, *Cynthia's Revels*   [2] R. Cotgrave, *Dictionary*, 1611.

In 1660 Pepys wrote:

'Calling at my father's to change my long black cloak for a short one, long cloaks being now quite out.'

Hats were worn out of doors but they were also worn indoors for formal occasions and at meals (Fig. 14). Pepys wrote in 1664:

'Got a strange cold in my head by flinging off my hat at dinner.'   Sept. 22nd

The shapes are best seen in the illustrations.

The tall crowned Tudor hat known as the *Copotain* continued till 1620 and was revived from 1640 to about 1655, when it was called the *Sugar loaf hat*. The Cavalier hat was large and often feather-trimmed (Fig. 15).

The three-cornered hat came into fashion after 1690.

Caps were unfashionable and only worn for comfort; for example, the night cap was worn by day as négligé. The *biggin*, close-fitting with ear flaps, was worn at night and also by children.

Hair styles (Fig. 16) varied as follows:

(1) Close curls and a clean-shaven face.

(2) A short pointed beard and moustache, and short hair.

(3) Long flowing locks.

A writer in 1628 said:

'Your gallant is no man unless his haire be of the woman's fashion, dangling and waving over his shoulders.'

The *love-lock* was also worn by 'gallants' until Charles II's reign. It was a tress of hair curled over one shoulder to fall in front. Some dandies wore two, one on each side.

1665–1700

From about 1665 a great change took place in men's fashions. The doublet and jerkin began to be replaced by coat and waistcoat, terms which have been used ever since. *The coat* at first hung loosely to the knees (Fig. 17). It had back and side vents, no collar and was buttoned all down the front. The sleeves were elbow-length with large turn-back cuffs and pockets were set very low (Fig. 18). After 1680 the coat was more figure-fitting with sleeves to the wrist and pockets raised. A countrified jacket called a 'jump' was worn by peasants (Fig. 19).

The waistcoat was cut like the coat, but always a little shorter so as not to show below. (*See* Fig. 17.) It was sometimes worn alone. Pepys wrote in 1666:

'I have of late taken too much cold by . . . going in a thin silke waistcoat, without any coate over it.'   June 20th

The most important new *neck wear* was the *cravat*. It was a short lace-edged linen or muslin scarf tied in a bow under the chin or having the ends tied together with the cravat string which was coloured ribbon, also tied in a bow. It has been said that:

'James II paid £36.10.0 for a cravat of Venice lace to wear on the day of his coronation.'

Leg Wear

Bloomer-like breeches fastened above or more often below the knee were usual (*see* Fig. 19). Towards the end of the century they were better fitting and fastened below the knee. They were cut so as to cling round the hips, as braces had not yet come into use.

19

A curious short-lived fashion must be mentioned, lasting from 1660–70. This was the fashion for *petticoat breeches* introduced from France and much favoured by Charles II for Court wear, but not much liked by the average Englishman. Petticoat breeches had extremely wide knee-length legs gathered into a waistband and the general appearance was that of a skirt. They were lavishly trimmed with ribbon loops called 'fancies' all round the waist and sometimes on the outer sides of the hem (Fig. 21).

Pepys wrote of a friend who had taken to wearing petticoat breeches and

'told of his mistake the other day, to put both his legs through one of the knees of his breeches and went so all day'.

1661, April 6th

EXTRAS

Embroidered gauntlet gloves were very fashionable, and perfumed gloves too were popular (Fig. 22).
A bridegroom wrote in 1642:

'I shall want a paire of plaine perfumed gloves for myselfe.'[1]

Long and short walking sticks or canes as they were called, rapiers, daggers and swords were also part of a gentleman's outfit.
Muffs were also carried by gentlemen. Pepys wrote in the winter of 1662:

'This day I first did wear a muffe, being my wife's last year's muffe.'

[1] Oxinden Letters.

1. Doublet, an original specimen worn by James I (*c.* 1603). Can be seen at the Victoria and Albert Museum.

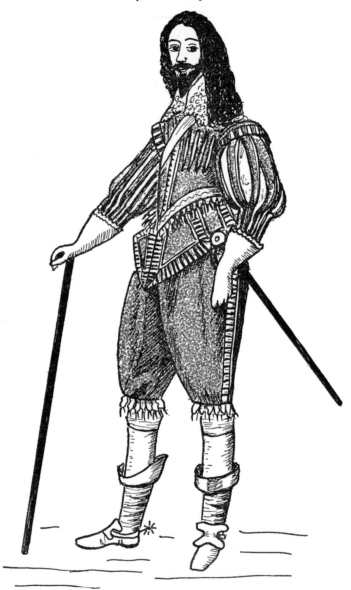

2. Charles I wearing a doublet with 'paned' sleeves. He also has a shoulder belt and wears cloak bag breeches (see p. 16) trimmed with aglets, metal tags. He wears gauntlet gloves and carries a stick and a sword. 1631.

3. Sir Walter Raleigh in a sleeveless jerkin with wings, worn over a doublet buttoned up the front. Trunk hose with canions and stockings pulled up over them, gartered with sash garters below the knee.
His son in doublet, breeches and a turndown collar called a falling band.
1602.

4. Scribe wearing gown with hanging sleeves. 1632.

5. (a) A compound ruff. (b) a falling ruff, (c) a small falling band, (d) a wide falling band (typical of the 1630's. Cf. fig. 15 (c) and 39).

6. Trunk hose without canions. Also doublet with wings and
a standing band and cuffs to match. 1616.

7. Venetians, also knee-length cloak. 1610.

8. Cloak bag breeches. 1625. (See also Fig. 2.)

9. Charles II aged 11. Long Spanish breeches. Large ribbon bows to sash garters, large shoe roses, cloak, and hat in hand. 1641.

10. Men in Dutch breeches, one with magnifying glass, the other making spectacles. 1664. The original caption reads: 'A flea-appeareth in a Multiplying-glass like a little pigg.' 1664.

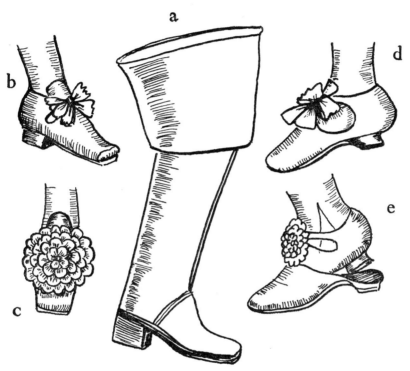

11. Footwear: (a) bucket-top boot *c.* 1645.
                 (b) square toe and shoe tie *c.* 1640.
                 (c) shoe rose *c.* 1635.
                 (d) round toe *c.* 1610.
                 (e) shoe and pantofle *c.* 1624.

12. Schoolmaster wearing a fashionable cloak, coat, and
Dutch breeches.
Boy wearing a short doublet and Dutch breeches. 1664.

13. First horseman in a sleeved cloak, second in a gaberdine.
1662–3.

14. Men and women wearing headgear during a meal. 1675.

15. Hats and caps: (a) embroidered 'night cap', (b) and (d) tall-crowned hats, (c) Cavalier hat (Prince Rupert). 1635.

16. Hair styles and cravats:
   (a) long wig. Note the shoulder knot. 1671.
   (b) love-locks. 1665.
   (c) natural hair simulating a wig, 1680–90.
   (d) long French wig. 1695–1700.

17. New style coat and
waistcoat. 1668–70.

18. Angler in fashionable coat, low
pocket, short sleeves and cuff turned
back; shoulder knot. 1671.

36

19. Peasant wearing a jump, very full breeches and short boots called 'startups'. 1672.

20. Horseman and groom. Gentleman in riding coat, plumed hat and top boots. Groom's coat is shorter than the fashion and his hat has no feather.
1686.

21. Charles II in petticoat breeches trimmed with many ribbon
loops. Large turnover tops to his boot hose. 1662.

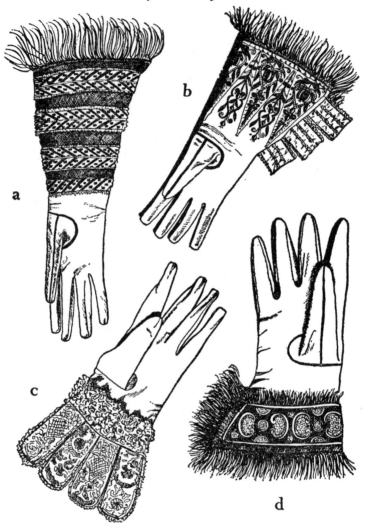

22. Gloves: (a) long gauntlet embroidered and fringed, *c.* 1602.
            (b) embroidered gauntlet with ribbon loops, *c.* 1625–50.
            (c) gauntlet with embroidered tabs, 1600–25.
            (d) embroidered and fringed, 1630–40.

WOMEN'S CLOTHES

As with the men, the 16th century styles, with modifications, continued until about 1625.

A lady's dress consisted of a tight boned bodice buttoned or tied with ribbon bows down the front, or made with a gap in front which was filled in by a *stomacher*. This was a panel somewhat V-shaped, with the point ending at the waist. It was boned and often embroidered. The bodice could be high-necked or just high at the back and very low in front, so low sometimes that there was actually a fashion among unmarried women for exposing the breasts.

The sleeves were either tight to the wrist or distended with padding or even with whalebone hoops sewn into the lining. Hanging sleeves were sometimes added and wings were usual.

The skirt, always joined to the bodice, varied in shape according to what was worn underneath it. The old-fashioned *farthingale* was usual until the 1620's (Fig. 23). This was a rigid petticoat, distended with hoops of whalebone, wood or wire. The largest was the *wheel farthingale* which spread out horizontally all round from the waist and gave the skirt a tub-shaped look. To soften the hard line produced when the skirt dropped straight down from the edge of the wheel, many skirts were made with deep frills spreading from the waist to the rim. These were known as 'frounced' skirts.

The *roll farthingale*, popularly known as the *bumroll*, was quite different. It was a padded roll shaped something like a life belt and worn just below the waist. It was open in front where it was tied by tapes. A writer in 1600 called it 'A boulster for their Buttocks.'[1] Farthingales were not always worn even while fashionable. Lady Anne Clifford wrote in her Diary in 1617:

'All the time I was at Court I wore my green damask gown without a farthingale.'

Most working women did not use them.

The word gown implied a woman's dress, but it was also used at this date for a loose garment, often sleeveless or with hanging sleeves, and generally worn over the dress, having a jacket bodice (Fig. 24). A garment called a *night gown* was worn as négligé for comfort by day! (Fig. 25.) All through this century the *jacket* or waistcoat, that is a short coat to the waist or hips, was an unboned and more comfortable alternative kind of bodice. The sleeves were long and close fitting and always with wings. There were some new styles after 1625. The bodice was less rigid, shorter waisted and sometimes made with *basques* (Fig. 26a). The sleeves were often very full and distended with horse-hair. Some were tied round in the middle with ribbon so as to make two balloon shapes known as 'virago sleeves'. The skirt, no longer distended by a farthingale, was full, ground length and often trained. Some skirts were open in front to show an elegant underskirt (Fig. 26b). In the last half of this century this kind of skirt was very popular and in the 1680's some women wore bustles.
Long waisted bodices then returned and a small waist was considered essential. These bodices had elbow-length sleeves edged with ruffles (Fig. 27).

[1] S. Rowland, *Satyr 7*.

Women's Clothes

Women's neck wear varied. Like the men they might wear ruffs until these went out of fashion in the 1640's. Women's ruffs, however, were adapted to the styles of bodice worn. They were often open in front to show the neck and fan-shaped ruffs spreading round the back of the head were worn with low-necked bodices. There were, however, two kinds of ruffs worn by women only, not by men. One was an *oval ruff* spreading sideways over the shoulders (Fig. 28); the other was the *fan-shaped* ruff with a neck-line frill inside, a feature of the 17th century only (Fig. 29). Country workers avoided stiff ruffs altogether.

Collars called bands like those worn by men were also fashionable but new styles came in after 1625. Some took the form of large white-lace-edged handkerchiefs folded round the shoulders like a small shawl. They were called *neckerchiefs.* Another kind, very popular in the second half of the century, was a deep white collar falling round a low-necked bodice, and called a falling whisk. (*See* Fig. 27.)

A tucker was a narrow white fill-in for a low-necked bodice. At the wrist turn-back cuffs were usual or, with the shorter sleeves, ruffles.

Women's shoes and stockings were like those worn by men but boots were usual for riding.

The *raised heel* which came in with James I was very popular with women from then on. Heels were often made of cork. 'You shall see their cork heels fly up high," wrote a dramatist in 1611[1] (Fig. 30).

Mules too were very fashionable, that is shoes with toe caps only. *Pattens*, which were wooden soles raised on iron rings and strapped on over the ordinary shoe, were worn by

[1] Thomas Middleton, *The Roaring Girl.*

43

country women to raise them out of the mud and dirt of the roads. Chopines (very rare) did the same.

Out of doors women sometimes wore long overcoats, but cloaks were more usual. *Shoulder capes* called *tippets* were worn indoors and out for warmth (Fig. 31). Towards the end of the century hip-length riding coats often trimmed with fur were more popular. For riding, also, a *safeguard* was worn. It was an over-skirt to protect the riding habit from dirt.

Before describing headwear, it is interesting to note that for women to go bare-headed out of doors as well as indoors was fashionable all through the 17th century. This was very different from the centuries that followed.

Equally most kinds of headgear could be worn in or out of doors. *Sugar loaf hats* with tall crowns were worn (Fig. 32); also hats with very wide brims. Hoods called *chaperones* (*see* Fig. 34) were worn out of doors only. *Coifs* were close-fitting small bonnets, white or embroidered in colours. These were indoor wear, but were often worn out of doors under a hat.

'Hoods by the whole dozens White and Black
And store of Coifs she must not lack.'[1] 1690

Lace-trimmed caps of different shapes were also worn. The head rail was a style falling down behind (Fig. 33). The *fontange* (*see* Figs. 25 and 43b, was a French fashion which only came in about 1690. It had a tall erection of lace or linen frills in front joined to a small cap at the back of the head with two dangling streamers. A *bongrace* (*see* Fig. 29), was a stiffened strip of material placed flat on the head and projecting over the forehead, supposed to protect the complexion from the sun. It was not very successful and soon went out of fashion.

[1] John Evelyn, *Mundus Muliebris.*

44

Apparently a more successful contrivance was the *mask*, which was used throughout the century (Fig. 34). The whole mask was oval in shape with holes for the eyes, nose and mouth; the half mask covered the eyes only. Both were also worn as a disguise.

A *muffler* in this century was a fold of material worn over the mouth and chin and not round the neck (Fig. 35). It went out of fashion in Charles II's reign.

Hair styles are best understood from the illustrations (Figs. 36 and 37). Wigs were sometimes worn. Hair decorations with ribbon bows called knots were very popular. The top knot was a large bow worn on the top of the head.

The wearing of *make up* with paint, powder and rouge was widely practised and black patches, though sometimes used earlier, became the fashion from 1640 to the end of the 18th century. This is how they were described at that time.

'Your black patches you wear variously, some cut like stars, some in half moons, some in lozenges.'[1]
They were supposed to show up the whiteness of the complexion (Fig. 38).

Towards the end of this century curious so-called aids to beauty were *Plumpers*. These were small cork balls placed inside each cheek:

'to plump out and fill up the cavities of the cheeks'.

An unfortunate thing happened to one lady who was wearing them.

'With one blow of her fist she not only made several of her

[1] John Fletcher and Philip Massinger, *The Elder Brother*.

D

45

teeth leap out of her mouth, but also two little cork Plumpers which served to fill out her hollow jaws.'[1]

The teeth may have been false teeth, as they were now being worn for show to fill up gaps in front, but they were no use for chewing.

EXTRAS

Gloves, short or elbow-length, and long silk gloves for full evening dress, often scented, were the fashion. Mittens were worn in the summer and muffs in cold weather.

Aprons, though common with working housewives, were also worn by grand ladies, but their aprons had no bibs and were made of fine material.

Fans and mirrors too were in constant use, and ladies were very proud of their lace-edged handkerchiefs.

> 'Of pocket mouchoirs Nose to drain
> A dozen lac'd, a dozen Plain.' 1690

---

[1] Baronne d'Annoy's Travels (trans.).

23. Dress with a close-fitting bodice, tight sleeves and hanging sleeves, a frounced farthingale skirt. A standing band with cuffs to match. She holds a feather fan. *c.* 1603.

24. Short gown with hanging sleeves, worn over a jacket bodice.
Skirt not distended by a farthingale. *c.* 1600–1.

25. A night gown, a sort of day négligé. This lady wears
a fontange. 1694.

26. (a) New style; bodice and skirt, the bodice with basques.
    Mirror suspended from belt. 1640.
    (b) Gown with open skirt, elegant underskirt. Bodice with
    'virago' sleeves. 1628. See also Figs. 33 and 42.

27. Tight, boned bodice, short sleeves, edged with ruffles, open skirt showing embroidered underskirt. This kind of lace collar was called a falling whisk. 1670–80.

51

28. Oval ruff. 1640.

29. Fan-shaped ruff with inner frill. This lady wears
a bongrace. *c.* 1605.

30. Shoes: (a) chopine. 'Your Ladyship is nearer heaven than when I saw
you last by the altitude of a chopine' 1603. *Hamlet*: (b) shoe and embroidered clog: (c) shoe with pointed toe and high heel: (d) mule: (e) patten.

31. Tippet (cape) and apron. 1688.

32. A sugar-loaf hat over a coif, a lace-edged neckerchief
and open skirt showing elegant underskirt. *c.* 1645.

33. A head rail and a gown with
'virago' sleeves. 1639.
(Kneeling effigy.)

34. Lady wearing a half mask, also
a chaperone (hood), a fur stole
and a muff. 1644.

35. Lady wearing a muffler. 1611.

36. Hair style. 1652.

37. Hair style, 'Hurluburlu'. 1675–80.

Here be your new
Fashions Mistris.

38. Advertisement showing different shapes of black patches,
also whole mask and feather fan. 1656.

CHILDREN'S CLOTHES

Children were dressed like their parents (Figs. 42, 43). Little boys were dressed like girls (Figs. 39, 40) until the age of six or seven, when they were 'breeched', that is, given breeches instead of long skirts.

Although men had long hair, schoolboys were ordered to keep their hair short.

> 'Thy head let that be combed and trimmed
> let not thy hair grow long,
> It is unseemly to the eye,
> rebuked by the tongue.'
>
> (Richard Weste, 1619)

The same writer advised boys to be more particular about using handkerchiefs, generally called *muckinders*. (*See* Fig. 39.)

> 'Nor imitate with Socrates
> to wipe thy snivelled nose
> Upon thy cap, as he would do
> nor yet upon thy clothes.
>
> But keep it clean with handkerchief,
> provided for the same,

Hanging sleeves served as 'reins' with little children and were then called leading strings (see Fig. 39 and James in Fig. 42).

39. Boy aged 6 wearing a doublet and skirt. On his head he has a lace-edged coif, with matching cuffs and wide falling band. A leading string is shown hanging from his left shoulder and from his girdle dangles a muckinder (handkerchief). 1632.

40. Boy aged 7 dressed as a girl. 1680.

41. Boys at play in short doublets and Dutch breeches. 1658.

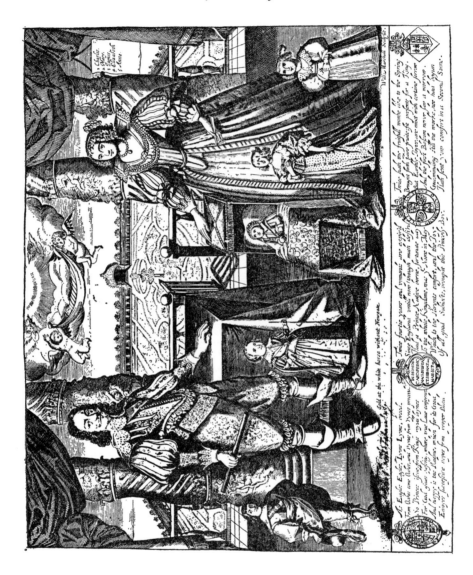

43. (a) Princess Mary Stuart aged 10 in a dress with stomacher front and open skirt. She has a lace-edged neckerchief, cuffs to match and a small tucker crossing the bosom. 1641.

---

42. (*See page 64*). Children of Charles I. From left to right: Charles aged *c.* 10 (later Charles II), dressed as an adult. Notice his sword and shoe roses. James aged 7 (later James II), wearing a doublet with leading strings and a long skirt. The baby Anne has a coif. Mary, aged *c.* 9, has a trained skirt and Elizabeth's hair style is like her mother's. *c.* 1640.

43. (b) Boy aged 7 and girl aged 3 dressed as fashionable grown-ups. The boy holds a 'tricorne' hat just coming into fashion. His cravat falls over stiffened cravat strings. The girl wears a trained gown with leading strings and a fontange head dress. 1695.

18th Century

INTRODUCTION

All through the 18th century, in spite of wars, there was a continuous interchange of fashions with France by means of dolls called 'moppets' dressed in the newest styles, and later by newspaper articles.

A foreign visitor wrote in 1722:

'The dress of the English is like the French but not so gaudy; they generally go plain but in the best cloths and stuffs. . . .'[1]

An unexpected thing happened in the development of men's fashions in this century. For the first time in the history of fashion gentlemen began to adopt styles worn by the working man. The most popular was a loose comfortable coat known as a frock (not a frock coat). The word frock was not used for a woman's dress until the end of the century.

In 1739 an observer of fashion wrote:

'There is at present a reigning ambition among our young gentlemen of degrading themselves in their apparel to the class of the servants they keep. . . .'[2]

Class distinction inherited from the past was just beginning to be undermined. This attitude was not favoured by the women.

A writer in 1775 observed:

[1] *The Universal Spectator.*
[2] *A Journey Through England,* ed. J. Macky.

69

'Whenever a thing becomes the mode it is universally adopted from the garret to the kitchen, when it is only intended for some very few Belles in the first floor.'[1]

From 1760 to 1780 there was an outburst of extravagance among the 'nobility and gentry' and as a protest against this a club was formed by young men who had travelled in Italy and brought back some new ideas about dress. They called themselves the *Macaronis*. Very soon, however, they themselves began to appear in fantastic costumes and were very much laughed at in contemporary writings (Fig. 44).

The 18th century showed an interest too in fashions of the past and aristocrats often had their portraits painted in so-called 17th century styles (a point to remember when visiting a portrait gallery).

Women, in particular, appear to have enjoyed this sort of revival, as shown in the hoop petticoats, reminiscent of the farthingales, and still later at the end of the century when they went to the opposite extreme and revived the Classical styles of Ancient Greece.

Generally speaking, however, 18th century fashions are picturesque and pleasing and fortunately many good specimens have been preserved and can be seen in some of our museums.

Children, as in the 17th century, were dressed like their parents, except that boys up to the age of six or seven still wore clothes like their sisters. After this they were 'breeched', that is put into breeches, or after 1790 they sometimes wore trousers.

[1] *London Magazine.*

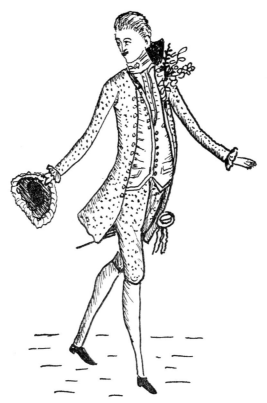

44. A Macaroni. '. . . in the present winter . . . the Macaroni gentlemen wear artificial nose gays—surely this species of animal is not an English character'. Letter written in April 1772.

MEN'S CLOTHES

A man's suit consisted of coat, waistcoat and breeches.

All through this century men's coats had no seam at the waist and two kinds were worn, the coat and the frock.

THE COAT

The coat (evening or day wear, or as they expressed it 'dress' or 'undress'). This was close-fitting to the waist, with a flared skirt to about knee level. It had a back vent and two side vents all topped with buttons. It had no collar until 1765. After that it had a stand collar.

During the first half of the century it was generally, though not always, buttoned from neck to hem, but after *c.* 1770, when it was gradually becoming a tail coat, the buttons ended at the waist. It had pockets with flaps, one on each side. *Sleeves with cuffs* were usual. There was one kind of cuff, very fashionable in the 1720's and 1730's, which reached up to the elbow. It was known as a boot cuff, and the sleeve called a boot sleeve (Fig. 45). Henry Fielding wrote in 1735:

'These boot sleeves were certainly intended to be the receivers of stolen goods and I wish the tayler had been hanged who invented them.'[1]

Sleeves without cuffs were called slit sleeves, as they had a slit down the outside.

[1] *The Miser.*

72

The Frock, for day wear especially, was worn from 1730. It was made like the coat, but was looser and more comfortable (Fig. 47). Its distinguishing feature was a turn-down collar. It was popular for sport and riding and was the usual wear of the working man, but from the 1770's men wore it on all occasions except at Court. An Englishman, in a letter from fashionable Paris, wrote in 1752:

'I was so damned uneasy in a full dressed coat with hellish long skirts. . . . I frequently sighed for my little loose frock which I look upon as an emblem of our happy constitution. . . .'[1]

Double-breasted frocks with lapels began to appear in the 1780's, though sometimes worn earlier for riding.

The Waistcoat (or Vest) was made like the coat but was always shorter so as not to show below the coat hem. It had slit sleeves, but never cuffs. After 1750–60 sleeves were given up, but sleeved waistcoats were worn as jackets, without coats, by servants to the end of the century. From the 1760's some waistcoats had small stand collars and lapels and in the 1790's they were all square cut at the base (see Fig. 48) instead of the Λ shape.

BREECHES

Knee breeches were the fashion all through the 18th century. They were buckled below the knee and stockings called *rollups* were pulled up over them (*see* Fig. 45). From about 1735, however, most men preferred to buckle over the stocking and rollups went out of fashion. At first, breeches were buttoned up in front, without having the buttons covered as with a fly closure.

[1] Arthur Murphy, *Grays Inn Journal*.

After 1730 they were closed with a turn-down flap called a *fall* (Figs. 48a and 48b). This might be small or what was known as a whole fall which covered the whole front. (*See* Fig. 79.)

In the 1790's *pantaloons* as an alternative to breeches came into fashion. Pantaloons were close-fitting tights ending near the ankles.

Trousers were not worn by civilians but only by soldiers, sailors and sometimes by labourers and also young boys. (*See* Fig. 79.) *Braces* called *Gallowses* began to be worn from about 1787.

As well as the coat belonging to the suit there were two long loose coats which men wore for comfort indoors. One was called a *night gown,* but was never worn in bed; the other a *morning gown* (Fig. 49). Both had wrap-over fronts and re-sembled dressing gowns. The morning gown was closer fitting and occasionally worn out of doors.

'Sometimes in slippers and a morning gown
He pays his early visits round the town.'[1]   1748

The *Indian night gown* or *banyan* was another garment for home wear. It was shorter, usually about knee length and a little smarter (Fig. 50).

These three garments were usually worn with 'night caps', which were comfortable caps for day wear indoors.

At the end of the century the banyan was very popular and sometimes worn out of doors. The *Town and Country Magazine* wrote in 1785:

'Banyans are worn in every part of the town, from Wapping

[1] Soame Jenyns, *Poems.*

74

to Westminster. . . . This however is the fashion, the ton, and what can a man do? he must wear a banyan.'

NECK WEAR

The word neckcloth or neckcloths was used all through this century and meant any kind of neck wear.

The cravat was a strip of linen, lawn or muslin tied round the neck and knotted under the chin; the falling ends were generally edged with lace. It went out of fashion in the 1740's. From 1785 the cravat came back into fashion in the form of a length of muslin wound three times round the neck and tied in a knot under the chin.

The stock came into fashion about 1730 and lasted all through the century. It was a high neckband of linen or cambric, often stiffened with pasteboard and buckled behind.

A black military stock was often worn by sporting young men.

FOOT WEAR

Shoes were buckled over broad tongues, and had square toes and high heels. After 1740 the toes were rounded and heels lowered. Shoes laced up instead of buckled were not worn by men.

Slippers for indoor wear were often like mules.

Pumps were shoes with thin soft soles and popular with acrobats and runners.

Boots were chiefly worn for riding, hunting and travelling. There were three kinds:

(1) *Heavy jack boots* were made of very strong leather with bucket-shaped tops and they reached above the knee. They were worn for riding (Fig. 51).

(2) *Light jack boots* were shaped to the leg, covered the knee in front, but were scooped out behind to allow for bending the knee (Fig. 52).

Hessians were short riding boots rising to a point in front to below the knee and generally decorated with a tassel. (Introduced in the 1790's.)

(3) *Half Boots*, often called jockey boots, ended below the knee with a turn-down top of a lighter colour.

Highlows were short ankle-length boots laced up in front. They were very like the 'Startups' of the early 17th century. Highlows were mostly worn by country folk and workmen from about 1750 onwards.

Stockings, often knitted in bright colours, were very fashionable. White was correct for both men and women at weddings.

Spatterdashes were gaiters of canvas or leather, reaching above the knee and spreading over the foot, secured by an under-instep strap. They were laced, buckled or buttoned down the outside.

OUTDOOR GARMENTS

The chief out-of-doors garment now for men was a *great coat*, often called a *surtout*, and from 1738 sometimes known as a *wrap-rascal* (Fig. 53). It was a large loose overcoat reaching to below the knees. Some had side vents, but always a back vent when worn on horseback. It was much beloved by coachmen. It had a small collar round the neck and one, two or three cape-like collars below this to shed the rain (Fig. 54b). The *Ipswich Journal* in 1749 described a highwayman wearing 'a double-breasted light coloured great coat with a blue-grey frock and scarlet waistcoat'.

In 1790 a short waist-length jacket called a *Spencer* came

into fashion for country wear (Fig. 54a). It had a roll collar and cuffs and was buttoned down the front.

Cloaks were worn until about 1750 but after that they were only correct for the army, the learned professions and at funerals.

HEAD WEAR

The three-cornered hat (called a tricorne in the 19th century) was fashionable all through the 18th century. The brim was cocked, that means turned up, on three sides, giving the hat a triangular shape, and it was worn with the point in front. There were many variations and different styles had different names. They were sometimes trimmed with cockades, or braid of silver or gold, or feathers round the edge of the brim. Because of the discomfort of wearing a hat over a wig many were just carried under the arm, but it was not correct to be seen out of doors without a hat.

In the 1770's an alternative style came into fashion, called the *Round hat*. (*See* Figs. 48b, 54 and 79). This was a round flat-topped crown and a round flat brim—a complete change.

Jockey caps—peaked and black—were sometimes worn on horseback.

Night caps, close-fitting and often embroidered, were worn by day over the bald head when the wig was removed for comfort. Artists often wore night caps and night gowns when at work. Soft, rather shapeless night caps were worn in bed and also by labourers out of doors. You can see some good examples of night caps as worn by an artist, on the splendid busts of Hogarth in the National Portrait Gallery.

HAIR

Wigs were worn by all men throughout this century and the

F

face was clean-shaven. A foreign visitor to England in 1748 wrote:

'Men all wore them (wigs), farm servants, clod-hoppers, day labourers . . . in a word all labouring folk go thro' their every day duties all with perukes on their heads.'

P. Kalm, On his visit to England in 1748.

If a man could not afford a wig (they were expensive) he dressed his hair in the style of whatever wig happened to be fashionable, and there were a great many. Roughly speaking wigs can be divided into two classes—those with pig tails or queues as they were called, and those without.

(1) *Tie wigs* had queues of varying length and were tied with a bow at the nape of the neck. (*See* Figs. 46 and 55b.) Barristers wear similar wigs today.

(2) *The Major wig* had two short queues (Fig. 55a).

(3) *The bagwig* was a dress wig. The queue was enclosed in a black silk bag which was tied with a large black bow at the back of the neck. This wig was often referred to as a *bag*. It is important to note this, as it can be confusing if you come across the word in 18th century literature when it doesn't mean a hand bag.

Wigs without queues were very varied.

(1) The *full-bottomed* or Full bottom wig (1660 to early 18th century) had a centre parting and was made up of masses of curls falling down round the shoulders (Fig. 56). After 1730 it was chiefly worn by the learned professions and courtiers.

(2) *The bob wig* could be short or long. The short bob left the neck uncovered, the long bob covered the neck behind. They too were curly.

(3) *The physical wig* was like a very bushy long bob and was

78

largely worn by physicians and surgeons. Tobias Smollett always wore one.

There were many other kinds of named wigs, too numerous to describe here.

The toupée or foretop, however, must be mentioned as fashionable men were very particular about their toupées. The foretop or toupée was the arrangement of the front hair above the forehead. This came into fashion in 1730 when centre partings were given up. A gentleman in 1740 feared 'to put on his hat, lest he should depress his foretop'.[1] Strange to say feathers were often used in the make-up of foretops, especially for parsons' wigs.

Wigs were made of human hair (the most expensive) also goats' hair, cows' hair and hair from calves' and foxes' tails. Textiles such as mohair, worsted and silk were also used and even copper and iron wire in spiral curls.

Wigs were usually powdered white or grey for dress wear, but black tie wigs were usual for riding. Other colours used were brown, flaxen and blue.

EXTRAS

Gloves were much plainer than in the 17th century and generally ended at the wrist. Gauntlet gloves, called 'high topped gloves', went out of fashion after 1750 except for riding.

Hedging gloves of stout leather were worn by countrymen and labourers.

Muffs were carried by gentlemen in cold weather. At first they were small but by the 1740's they were often very large (Fig. 57). Oliver Goldsmith in *The Bee* wrote:

[1] Samuel Richardson, *Pamela*.

'I can never get you to dress like a Christian . . . with your monstrous muff. I hate those odious muffs.'   1765

A sword was worn, even on horseback. It was said in 1754 that:

'The grand distinguishing mark of a fine gentleman is the wearing of a sword.'[1]

Swords were forbidden to working men from 1710.

Walking sticks, generally called *canes*, were also carried.

In 1756 Jonas Hanway introduced the *umbrella*, but Englishmen, at first, considered this to be unmanly.

Handkerchiefs might be white or coloured. Silk handkerchiefs, generally coloured, were used by snuff takers and often called snuff handkerchiefs.

Make-up in the 18th century was practised by dandies. In fact it was said that the *Beau* took as much pains as the *Belle* over this. He used rouge, lipstick and eyebrow painting, and some even put on patches. He padded out his legs if his calves were thin and used plenty of scent. This was partly to overcome the smell of beer and tobacco which clung to his clothes.

Watches were a favourite form of jewellery; two were often carried, one sometimes being sham. It was either dangled from the fob pocket of the breeches or carried in it. A beau was described in 1777 as wearing 'a ring, two watches and a snuff box gilt'.[2]

[1] *The Connoisseur*, 1754.
[2] *Universal Magazine.*

45. Coat, with boot cuffs, waistcoat and roll-up stockings. 1720.

M·CHARTA

JOHN WILKES Efq^r. *1768.*

46. John Wilkes in collarless coat, breeches buckled
below the knee and buckled shoes. 1768.

82

47. (*left*) Gentleman wearing a frock, i.e. a coat with a turn-down
collar, and a waistcoat of fashionable length. 1760.
48. (*right*) Two men rather ashamed of their umbrellas. (Introduced
for men by Jonas Hanway in 1756.)
   (a) has a three-cornered hat and pigtail wig,
   (b) has a round hat, a long frock, square cut waistcoat and
      breeches closed by a 'fall'. 1782.

49. Artist wearing a morning gown, also called night gown, night cap, and mules on his feet. *c.* 1740.

50. Banyan, night cap and slippers. 1735.

B.C.P.

51. Heavy jack boots for riding, worn by Charles Tottenham, M.P., nick-named 'Boots' from the occasion when in order to be in time to vote he failed to remove these on entering the House. *c.* 1745.

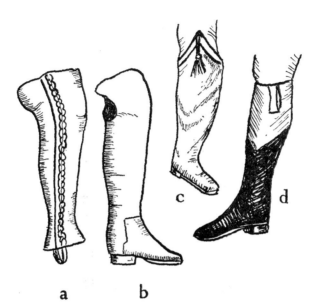

52. Boots: (a) long spatterdash,
     (b) light jackboot,
     (c) Hessian,
     (d) top boot or jockey boot.

B.C.P.

53. Dr. Johnson in his 'brown cloth great coat' with deep pockets. Jockey boots and 'a large English oak stick'. 1773.

54. (*left*) A Spencer.
   (*right*) A greatcoat with multiple collars. (Caricatures.) 1792.

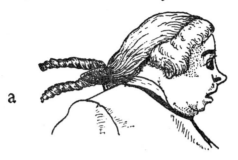

55. (a) A Major wig. 1755.
    (b) A Tye-wig. 1772.

56. Sir Christopher Wren wearing a full-bottomed wig. *c.* 1700.

57. A dandy carrying a muff, a cane, a sword and a tricorne hat. He wears a long pigtail wig, and roll-ups. 1746.

WOMEN'S CLOTHES

All through the 18th century a woman's dress had three main styles, which for convenience we will call the open robe, the closed robe and the separate bodice and skirt style. A skirt at this time was always called a petticoat and, confusingly, sometimes shortened to 'coat'.

(1) *The open robe* had a bodice and skirt joined at the waist, but the skirt was open in front to show an elegant underskirt, also called a petticoat, but it was not an undergarment in the modern sense.

(2) *The closed robe* had no opening in the skirt.

(3) *The separate bodice and skirt.* In this style the bodice was always in the form of a close-fitting waisted jacket. Some low-necked bodices were open in front and the gap was filled in by a *Stomacher*, which was a panel, usually embroidered, with a straight border above and sloping to a point at the waist. *Sleeves* were about elbow length and finished with cuffs at first but later with flounces and white frills called ruffles. (*See* Fig. 58.) Long sleeves did not come into fashion until the 1780's, except for a gown called the German gown, which had long sleeves in 1760. The skirt, until about 1710, was full, long and often trained. From 1710 to 1780 (and to 1820 for Court wear) the hang of the skirt depended on the shape of the *hooped petticoat*, or *hoop* as it was called, which was worn underneath. This was a rigid under-petticoat distended with hoops

of cane, wire or whalebone. Dome-shaped hoops were worn all through this period.

A lady wrote in 1780:

'I went to ball at Court the 15th last June. The assembly was not very numerous, but the ladies wore such large hoops that one of them kept as much room as four people like me—you know I am not very fat. I laughed about it the next morning with the General. He told me it was the fashion—a foolish one indeed! When the princes wanted to do the Allemande they could not reach the ladies' hands.'

(Benendon Letters 1753–1821)

From the 1740's to the 1760's a hoop called the *oblong hoop* came into fashion (Fig. 58). It was flattened in front and behind, but spread out on each side, giving enormous breadth to the hips.

Let us now look at the more important styles of gown under the headings given.

THE OPEN ROBE

(1) The most famous was the *Sack* or *Sack-back* gown which was fashionable from 1720 to 1780 (Fig. 59). The back of this gown had box pleats stitched down on each side of the back seam from the neck to about shoulder level and then left loose to merge with the fullness of the skirt below.

(2) *The Polonese* was the height of fashion from 1770 to about 1785 when bustles, called false rumps, were worn. They were often made of cork. The distinguishing feature was the bunching up and puffing out of the overskirt behind the waist, completely uncovering the underskirt which was worn much shorter than usual (Fig. 70).

The Closed Robe

The wrapping gown was very popular during the first half of the 18th century (Fig. 60). The bodice had a wrap-over front which was continuous with the skirt. It was usually fastened at the waist with a brooch or ribbon and was worn with any hoop in fashion.

The riding coat dress (from 1785). (Fig. 61.) Although this was worn on horse-back it was also fashionable as a morning walking dress. It resembled a great coat with a falling collar, but was pulled in round the waist and buttoned all down the front to foot level. It had long tight sleeves. (*See also* Fig. 69b.)

The Separate Bodice and Skirt Style

With these dresses the skirts were always closed and the bodice was in the form of a jacket. These jackets had different names; the commonest only can be given.

(1) *The Petenlair* (1745–70's) was a thigh-length jacket with a sack-back, its distinguishing feature.

(2) *The Caraco* was a thigh-length jacket shaped to the figure, but without a seam at the waist.

(3) *The riding habit*. This was a dress with a riding coat and waistcoat, made like a man's but shaped to the female figure, and a long skirt (Fig. 62).

The Classical Dress of the 1790's

What has been termed the *Classical Style* appeared at the end of the 18th century, in the 1790's, when a great change took place. All dresses, apart from court wear, were high-waisted (Fig. 63). A paper in 1796 wrote:

94

Women's Clothes

'The Ladies' waists have ascended to their shoulders.'[1]

Skirts were straight, long and sometimes trained. Dresses were often of thin material even in the winter and many underclothes were left off. Everyone tried to look tall and slender and 'Grecian'.

NECK WEAR

The most usual was the handkerchief. The old word neckerchief though much more descriptive was going out and handkerchief meant neckwear unless pocket handkerchief was specifically stated. These handkerchiefs were folded cornerwise and draped round the neck. Some were cut in half and called half handkerchiefs. Towards the end of the century they were much larger and spread out over the shoulders like a shawl.

The tucker was a white edging to a low-necked bodice.

The modesty piece was a strip of lace or linen used as a fill-in for a low-necked bodice.

Small ruffs or ribbon neck bands were fashionable from about 1710 and short white shoulder capes called *Tippets* were worn throughout. A long cape called a *night rail* (late 17th to early 18th century), was essentially an indoor garment, though sometimes worn out of doors, unfashionably (Fig. 64).

Cravats like those worn by men were also worn by women riders.

FOOTWEAR

All through the first three-quarters of this century women's shoes were generally made with latchets, tied or buckled over

[1] *Chester Chronicle.*

95

a tongue. The toes at first were pointed and the heels very massive and high. The uppers were often embroidered when made of silk.

In 1730 Jonathan Swift wrote:

'By these embroidered high-heeled shoes
She shall be caught as in a noose;
So well contrived her toes to pinch
She'll not have power to stir an inch!'

Towards the end of the century the heels were less massive and some shoes had wedge heels (Fig. 65).

In the classical period the *sandal shoe* was introduced. This had a flat heel, was open over the foot and fastened by criss-cross ribbons over the instep and round the ankle.

Over-shoes called *clogs* are best understood by the illustrations. They were quite different from modern clogs.
Pattens had wooden soles raised on iron rings and were mostly worn in the country.

'The milk maid safe through driving rains and snows
Wrapp'd in her cloke and propp'd on pattens goes.'[1]

1730

Boots began to be fashionable in the 1770's for riding and driving. They were either half boots like those worn by men, or short boots resembling highlows, like startups.
Stockings knitted in various colours reached above the knee.

'With the rude wind her rumpled garment rose
And shewed her taper leg and scarlet hose.'[2]   1714

[1] Soame Jenyns, *The Art of Dancing.*
[2] John Gay, *The Shepherd's Week.*

Garters were ribbon or silk bands, tied above or below the knee and were frequently woven with mottoes such as 'No search', as young fops liked to snatch them off a lady's leg to keep as a trophy.

OUTDOOR GARMENTS

Cloaks of all sorts were usual until the 1780's. Subsequently *Parisian cloaks* were fashionable (Fig. 66).

The mantle was a long cloak which generally had a hood attached (Fig. 67).

The cardinal was a three-quarter-length scarlet cloak.

The mantlet was a shoulder cape and the *pelerine* was also a shoulder cape, but with long ends which could be crossed over in front, passed round the waist and tied behind. (*See* Fig. 69.)

The pelisse from 1750 to 1800 was a long cloak with slits for the arms to come through. The word, however, from about 1800 was transferred to an overcoat.

Shawls began to be fashionable for outdoor wear in 1780.

Overcoats came in when hoops went out in the 1780's.

In the Classical period a short-waisted jacket called a *spenser* was very popular. It was figure-fitting and had long sleeves.

HEADWEAR

Some kind of headwear was worn by most women all through this century. Indoors white caps in different designs were the commonest. These are the principal ones.

The pinner (1700–40) was flat, often having two long streamers called lappets which hung down behind or were turned up and pinned on top.

The round-eared cap (1730–60) was like a bonnet curved round the face covering the ears. (*See* Fig. 58.)

97

The mob cap was an 'undress' cap worn throughout. At first it was bonnet-shaped with a puffed out crown and tied under the chin. The ties were known as 'kissing strings'. After about 1750 it was merely a large white cap with a frill and ribbon trimming round the puffed out crown. (*See* Figs. 73 and 79.)

Out of doors women nearly always wore their hats over day caps. Perhaps the most popular hat of all was the *Bergère* or *Milk-maid* hat which lasted from the 1730's (Fig. 68). It was a round hat with a low crown and wide brim and worn at different angles according to the hair style in fashion.

The *Witches' hat* with a pointed crown was another countrified hat popular in the 1740's.

When hair styles from the 1770's to 1790's became so large and complicated, hats did the same and illustrations will be clearer than descriptions of these fantastic hats worn at different angles.

'What an opinion our great grandchildren might be led to form of the ladies' heads towards the close of the eighteenth century, if any of the fashionable hats should happen to be preserved.'[1]

There is one hat, of special historic interest called the *Balloon hat* or the *Lunardi* or *Parachute* hat, named after Lunardi, the Italian aeronaut who was one of the first to make a balloon ascent in England, in 1784 (Fig. 69a). This hat had a puffed out slightly balloon-shaped silk crown and a wide brim. A writer in 1786 said:

'The whole was so prepared as to catch every gale of wind and erect itself from the face . . . hence no doubt its name of balloon.'[2]

[1] *The Lounger*, 1786.   [2] *The Lounger.*

Consequently it was a short-lived fashion.

In the Classical period hats were smaller and generally fitted on the head instead of balancing on the coiffure. They were also often worn with veils.

Hoods of various kinds were also worn. Some had capes. But in the early 1770's hoods went out of fashion. After this date the only popular hood was the *calash*, which was worn over any other head-dress as a protection from the weather. It was a very large hood of silk, built up with arches of cane. It could be taken off and folded up when not needed.

HAIR STYLES

At first, apart from court wear, hair arrangements were fairly simple, with plenty of curls, some false, and always leaving the forehead uncovered. Wigs were sometimes worn, especially on horseback.

In the 1760's the back hair was generally turned up to form a large bun.

In the 1770's height was the fashion with curls and false hair added all round (Figs. 70 and 71). The *Gentleman's Magazine* wrote in 1777:

> 'With Babel-towers of hair as high
> As if they meant to reach the sky.'

In the 1780's width was the fashion (Fig. 72). All these hair styles were built up on pads stuffed with horse-hair and called hair cushions. Plenty of false hair had to be added and all was fixed in place with hair-pins, combs and paste and then powder. The very elaborate 'heads' as they were called might be left untouched for some weeks and not only caused head-aches but developed lice!

In the 1780's simpler styles came in. Some ladies had fringes and some tried to imitate the Grecian style.

Hair ornaments, apart from caps, were often worn. *The top knot* was a favourite throughout. (*See* Fig. 59.) It was a bunch of brightly coloured ribbon loops.

'As lately at a rural Fair
I ey'd around the beauties there
With top knots, red and green and blue.'[1]   1735

In the 1770's women wore all sorts of strange ornaments, such as artificial (or real) flowers, fruit, and vegetables. Jane Austen mentioned in a letter written in 1799 that she had seen 'strawberries, grapes, cherries, plums and apricots' used to decorate ladies' heads.

Feathers too from the 1770's became more and more fashionable. They were usually ostrich feathers and were worn standing upright on the head (Fig. 73). *The Times* of 1795 tells us that:

'At all elegant Assemblies, there is a room set apart for the lady visitants to put their feathers on, as it is impossible to wear them in any carriage with a top to it. A young lady only ten feet high was overset in one of the late gales.'

Make-up and Aids to Elegance

Rouge was used for the face, lips and finger-nails and sometimes white paint for the neck. Eyebrows were arched and sometimes artificial eyebrows made of mouse skin were stuck on. (*See* Fig. 74.) One lady lost hers like this:

'Her eyebrows on the toilet lay
Away the kitten with them fled.'[2]   *c.* 1700

[1] *The Gentleman's Magazine.*   [2] Matthew Prior.

Patches as described in the 17th century were worn till about 1790. Masks too were sometimes used.

EXTRAS

Embroidered silk and fancy aprons were often part of a fashionable lady's attire (*see* Fig. 58) and folding fans were indispensable. They were often used to express a fine lady's feelings.

> 'Its shake triumphant, its victorious clap,
> Its angry flutter and its wanton tap.'[1]   1730

Gloves, mittens, muffs and *pocket handkerchiefs* were all in use and any oddments that had to be carried were put into a pocket, often embroidered, slung from the waist under the skirt. It was not until the end of the century that a form of handbag was introduced. It was called a *ridicule* or *indispensible.* (*See* Fig. 63.)

As the gay and picturesque fashions of the 18th century came to an end in the last decade, when all was scanty and skimpy, it is interesting to read in the *Chester Chronicle* of 1799 that:

> 'There is so little to be concealed at present,
> that there is scarcely room for any fashion at all.'

---

[1] Soame Jenyns, *The Art of Dancing.*

58. (*left*) Shows an open robe over an oblong hoop. The lady wears a round-eared cap, a transparent apron and holds a bergère hat. 1743–45.
59. (*right*) Lady in a sack back gown and ruffles to sleeve. On her head she has a top knot. 1761.

60. (*left*) Wrapping gown, worn over a dome-shaped hoop. 1740–50.
61. (*right*) Riding coat dress, tall hat and hair style of the 1790's. 1790.

62. Riding habit, coat, waistcoat and long skirt, also a
tricorne hat trimmed with
feathers. 1740–50.

63. Ladies in long high-waisted
dresses, holding 'indispensibles',
i.e. handbags. 1799.

a   b

64. Night rails worn by lady in the stocks and a jeering child.
c. 1702.

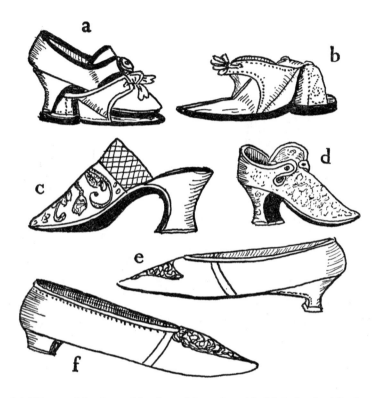

65. (a) Worn with clog; (b) clog; (c) mule with high heel; (d) shoe, *c.* 1700–30; (e) and (f) shoes of later period, *c.* 1785–95, with low heels and no latchets.

66. (*left*) Lady in a white muslin high-waisted dress and a pink
silk 'Parisian cloak' trimmed with black lace. 1799.
67. (*right*) A hooded mantle. 1721.

68. Bergère hat. 1750's.

a   b

69. (a) Balloon hat and a mantlet. 1789.
      (b) Back view of riding habit. 1789.

70. Very high hair style with decoration. The lady wears
a dress called a polonese. See p. 93. 1778.

71. Hair style of the 1770's.

72. Hair style and hat of the 1786's. (After a portrait of
Fanny Burney.)

73. Fashionable mother in 'nursing dress'. She has stylish tall feathers, gloves and a fan. Nurse wears a mob cap. 1796.

74. Please read the notice above the door of the cosmetic shop.
1782.

CHILDREN'S CLOTHES

75. Boy aged 3 dressed as a girl. 1766-7.

As with the 17th century, children were dressed much like their parents (Figs. 76-79) and little boys wore clothes like girls (Fig. 75). Little girls sometimes wore aprons and mob caps (Fig. 79).

76. Boy 'breeched', fashionably dressed. 1715. See Fig. 45.

77. Boy in the fashion, bowling his hoop. 1775. See Fig. 48.

78. Girl aged about 8 in long frock and large hat. 1787.

79. 'Black Monday.' Group: (a) Trousers (as worn by little boys only) with whole falls; a great coat or surtout. (b) His older brother in the more fashionable breeches. Both have round hats. (c) and (d) Mother and small girl wearing mob caps. 1790.

INDEX

Index